Math Is All Around Us

Math Is All Around Us

A Collection of Story Problems for Students and Teachers,
Grades 5-7

Gail Brown Slane

authorHOUSE®

AuthorHouse™
1663 Liberty Drive
Bloomington, IN 47403
www.authorhouse.com
Phone: 1-800-839-8640

Published by AuthorHouse   02/07/2012

ISBN: 978-1-4685-5200-3 (sc)
ISBN: 978-1-4685-5199-0 (ebk)

Library of Congress Control Number: 2012902542

Objectives

- The student will see that math is relevant in real-life situations.
- The student will become more confident applying math skills to different situations.
- The student will become more comfortable using math vocabulary.
- The student can practice math skills by applying them to real-life situations.
- The student can learn to apply problem solving strategies.
- The teacher can quickly assess a student's understanding of math concepts by assigning problems for class work or homework.

Author's Background

Gail Slane received her B.S. in Elementary Education from Appalachian State University, and she has taught a wide variety of grade levels over twenty years. She has taught in the United States and in Europe. She loves reading and traveling. She and her family live in Belleville, Illinois.

Contents

Add it Up

1. Last year, 62 students played in the band. This year, 14 more students play in the band. How many students play in the band this year?

2. On Thursday, 189 fifth graders visited the Washington Monument. On Friday, 248 sixth graders visited the monument. How many students went all together?

3. How many marbles between them would two boys have collected, if one had saved 64 and the other saved 356?

4. Is the sum of 258 and 874 greater or less than the sum of 997 and 290?

5. Marta sold 347 tickets on Monday and 259 tickets on Tuesday. How many tickets did she sell in all?

6. Allyse bought 3 biscuits at $.75 each and a loaf of bread for $2.79. How much did she spend in all?

7. Valerie made 30 cookies. Nick made 20 cookies. Alexander made 40 cookies. How many cookies were there in all?

8. John and Emily saw that there were 50 pencils in a box, 19 erasers and 15 sharpeners. How many things were in the box? Tell three facts about the number!

9. Kayla's mom spent $12.95 on Monday and $13.49 on Tuesday. How much did she spend in all?

10. Lillian had a student book with 80 sheets. Hannah had 120 sheets, and Laura had a notebook with 282 sheets. How many sheets did they have in all?

11. Courtney bought 3 pounds of bananas for $2.75, 2 bottles of water for $2.25, and she bought a team T-shirt for $19.95. She also bought jeans for $39.45. What is the sum of her purchases?

What's the Difference

1. On Friday, 264 people saw the movie. On Saturday, 345 people saw the movie. How many more people saw the movie on Saturday?

2. Hannah earned $6.50. She spent $3.79 for a book. How much money did she have left?

3. The motorcycle weighs 920 pounds. The 3-Wheeler weighs 1,680 pounds. Find the difference.

4. At the candy store, a Mars Bar costs $.60 and a six pack of Oreos cost $.95. How much more do the Oreos cost?

5. There were 765 bananas in the store. The manager had to toss out 469 because they were rotten. How many bananas were left?

6. If Jeff has $300.00 and he spends $158.53 on his school trip, how much will he have left?

7. Eric has $42.51. He wants to buy a computer game that costs $52.75. How much more does he need?

8. Jon ate 46 candy bars. James ate 60. How many more did James eat?
Do we know who would get sick faster? Do we know whose face would break out from all the sugar?

9. Alex had 597 kilograms of coal. He gave 146 kg to Jan and 123 to Dennis. How much did Alex give away? How much does he have left?

10. Elise's Used Cars has 23 Fords, 7 Mercedes, 20 Volkswagons and 37 Hondas. How many more cars does she need to have 100 cars?

11. Emre bought 5 CDs for $12.95 each. He also bought 2 games for $45.00 each. He gave the clerk $200.00. How much change did he get back?

12. Ceyda's family has $589.50 to spend on a new TV. The one they really want costs $899.68. How much more money do they need?

Giving and Taking Away

1. Jeff had 412 pounds of clay. He gave 138 pounds to Adam, and he gave 143 pounds to Ben. How much did Jeff give away?
How much clay does Jeff have left?

2. James went shopping. He bought a bag of tomatoes for $2.50 and 2 steaks for $5.46 each. How much did he spend?
How much change would he get back from $15.00?

3. Ben works 7 hours and 50 minutes on Monday, Tuesday, Wednesday and Thursday. He works just 4 hours on Friday so he can play golf all afternoon. How long does Ben work during the week? Does the information tell us if he won the game?

4. Eric bought a pair of headphones for $15.89 and 3 tapes for $7.89 each. Altogether, how much money did Eric spend?
Could he have bought 2 more tapes if he hadn't bought the headphones?

5. Anna bought 12 markers for $7.98, an easel for $9.45 and 10 pieces of extra-large poster paper for $12.00. How much did Anna spend? How much more did she pay for the paper than the easel?

6. Kaitlyn purchased a BBQ Sandwich for $2.95, fries for $.99 and a small drink for $.89. What was her final cost?
If she gave the clerk $10.00, how much change would Kaitlyn get back?

7. Three cows weighed a total of 1,076 kilograms. One weighed 332 kg, and another cow weighed 50 kg. How much did the third cow weigh? The _____ System uses kilograms!

8. There were 5,735 toys on the truck. One evening 3,591 were taken. How many toys were left in the truck?
List two facts about your number answer.

9. Travis bought a comb for $1.84, neon shoelaces for $3.49 and a new bike for $69.29. How much did Travis spend in all? How much change did he get back if he paid with a $100 bill?

10. Donovan had 46 movies. He lost 29 of them. He bought another 38 movies. How many movies was he left with? Why do you think he was losing so many movies?

11. Lillian rafted down 1,400 miles of one river. Kiersten rafted down a river that was 2,714 miles long. Find the sum and the difference of the numbers.

12. At the end of the first day of camp, Jeff counted 47 bites.
    The next morning he counted 114 bites! How many new bites did Jeff get? Explain why 114 is an even number.

13. There are 334 boys in the school and 289 girls. How many students attend the school? How many more boys are there?

14. There are 36 girls in the fifth-grade classes at the International School of Stuttgart. There are 5 more boys than girls.
    How many boys are there? What is the total number of students in 5th grade?

15. The Amazon River is approximately 4,000 miles long. The Mississippi River is approximately 2,347 miles long. How much longer is the Amazon River? Explain why 2,347 is an odd number.

Multiplication . . . Speedy Addition

1. The caterer baked 85 pies in a week. She sliced each into six pieces.
   How many pieces of pie did the caterer have?

2. Courtney packed 30 marbles into each rectangular box. She filled 49 boxes. How many marbles did Courtney pack?

3. When Kunal stood on his toes, he was 5 feet 11 inches tall. How many inches tall was Kunal when he stood on his toes?

4. Mrs. Slane will make pies for her 22 7th graders and her 15 6th graders.
   She will cut each pie into eight pieces. How many pies does she have to make in order for everyone to have a piece?

5. Michael worked at the ticket booth. He sold 129 tickets to the student-vs-teacher volleyball game. Each ticket was $1.25.
   How much money did Michael collect?

6. Malin is 62 inches tall. Help her convert this to centimeters (cm) by multiplying 62 by 2.54. Remember to place your decimal point back two places.

7. Rudolph noticed that each cracker had 15 holes in it. How many holes would 144 crackers have?

8. Rebecca bought 37 posters. Each poster cost $4.89. How much did she spend in all?

9. The monkeys eat 24 pounds of bananas each day. How many pounds will they eat in 14 days?

10. The Coppens planned to eat 14 meals while traveling. They budgeted $18 for each meal. How much did they budget for all their meals?

11. Shateria read where it takes 9 minutes per pound to defrost a turkey in the microwave. How long will it take to defrost a 25 pound turkey?

Multiplication Madness

1. Harley sneezed (7x8) + (41x49) – (4-2) times. How many times did she sneeze?

2. The bird collected string for 21 days. It collected 18 pieces each day. How many pieces of string did the bird collect in all?

3. Jean bought 4 mystery books for $6.85 each. How much did she spend?

4. Porcha, the puppy, earned 10 doggie treats a day for two weeks. How many treats did she earn?

5. Mr. Baker sold pieces of cake at the fair. He sold 124 pieces! Each piece was $.75. How much did Mr. Baker collect?

6. Kevin and Tim were playing "Name That Product" last night. Tim said the product of 815 and 3 was 240. Was Tim correct? If not, what is the correct answer?

7. Will saw 108 orange trees in a grove. Each tree had 95 buds on it. How many buds were on the orange trees?

8. The science teacher bought 50 new lab books. Each one cost $2.95. How much did she spend on lab books?

9. The baseball team needs to raise money to go to the capital for a championship game. They need to raise $250.00. They want to have a car wash. How many cars will they need to wash at $6.00 per car in order to achieve their goal?

10. Bill loves his ice-cream! He eats two small bowls a day. Each bowl has 210 calories in it. How many calories worth of ice-cream does Bill eat in a week?

11. The restaurant serves 11 ounce steaks. The manager needs 350 for tonight's meal. How much steak should be delivered to the restaurant?

12. Abby ate 650 scoops of ice cream in one week! At this rate, how many scoops will she eat in 6 weeks?

13. Lucy steps on 1,266 ants in a year. At this rate, how many will she step on in 5 years?

14. Harold flies approximately 7,000 miles each month. Approximately how far would he travel during 12 months?

15. Most of the fans who attended the baseball game came in 4 buses. Each bus held 70 people. How many fans rode the buses?

16. Each of the three jets that the students flew to get to France weighed 58,414 pounds. How much would three planes weigh?

17. Yushi loved reading his science book. He read 25 pages each day for a year. How many pages did he read in a year?
(Hint: 25 x 365)

18. Mary Ellen wrote a fiction book. She sold 98 to her friends and family. Each book was $6.95. How much money did she collect?

19. The local school will order 232 new math books. Each book costs $18.95. How much will the school spend on new math books?

20. Gauri earns $3.00 a day for an allowance. How much does she earn in a year?

21. Constantin, Joshua, Sophia, Seda and Anjelika each spent 18 hours working on their science fair project. How many hours did they spend in all on the project?

22. Help Niall and Malin find the answer to 49 x 42.

A Great Product

1. Coco's plant drops 6 leaves a day. At this rate, how many leaves will it drop during the year?

2. Mom already made a dozen (12) cookies. She is going to make 12 more sheets of a dozen. How many cookies will mom have after she is finished in the kitchen?

3. Christopher wanted to buy 25 Team Canada jerseys. Each costs $75.00. How much will he spend?

4. There are 130 children at Kent Middle School. How many pieces of pizza are needed if each child eats 3 pieces? If each piece costs $2.25, how much money will be needed to pay the pizza man?

5. A whale can swim 15 miles per hour. If it swims at this rate for 4 hours estimate how far it will swim.

6. Mr. Lawler ordered 24 books that cost $3.95 each, and he also ordered 16 workbooks that cost $4.95 each. How much did his order come to?

7. Eleven horses have _____ legs, _____ ears and _____ tails.

8. On Friday, 315 people visited the ISS Open House. On Saturday, 407 visited, and on Sunday 900 visited the Open House. If each person donated $2.50 to the school, how much money was collected?

9. The school band practices for 55 minutes each day. How many minutes will the band practice in 18 days?

10. Moyuru had 18 bundles of newspapers. Each bundle had 35 papers. How many papers did he have?

11. Victoria averages 65 miles per hour driving on the interstate. If she travels at this rate for 8 hours, how far will she travel?

12. Martina earned $25.00 for each lawn she mowed. If she mowed 12 lawns, how much would she earn?

Dividing It Up

1   Nine encyclopedias were stacked on a shelf. If 2 of the encyclopedias weigh a total of 64 ounces, all nine books weigh how many ounces?

2. The school bus holds 60 people. How many buses are needed to take 288 people on a field trip to the aquarium?

3. A total of 396 entries were received from 4 schools for the talent contest. How many entries were received from each school?

4. There were 231 people seated in 77 trucks along the road to watch the space shuttle land. How many people were in each truck?

5. The 5th grade teacher bought a total of 56 treats for the students to enjoy during a special drama presentation. He paid a total of $37.52. What was the cost of each treat?

6. Tom paid a total of $57.15 for 9 model kits. How much did he pay for each?

7. Helen and Vilma made pumpkin, cherry, peach and pecan pie.
    There are 32 students in their class. How many pieces should each pie be cut into?

8. Oliver ate 600 calories worth of Thin Mints that he got from Jessica. Each cookie was 40 calories. How many cookies did Oliver eat?

9. William spent $35.34 on pizzas. He got six. How much did each pizza cost?

10. How many 6-inch pieces of yarn can Sophie cut from an 86-inch piece? Will there be any left over?

11. Mr. C'Ya donated 29 books to the local library. He paid $377 for them. How much did each book cost?

12. A clown divided a bunch of 108 balloons evenly among 9 children. How many balloons did each child get?

13. Lucy was on Jeopardy. Alex said, "The answer when you divide." Lucy pressed the button quickly and yelled, "What is the _____ ?"

14. Ashley, Tessa and Maya drove 537 miles in one day.
    How far could they travel in 3 days at the same rate?
    If each girl drove the same distance per day, how many miles did they each drive?

15. Anton put 157 photographs in a photo album. He put 8 photos on each page. How many complete pages did Anton fill up?
    How many pictures were on another page?

16. One-hundred twenty students from around Germany participated in the Challenge Spelling Bee. Five schools were represented.
    How many students came from each school?

17. A total of 384 students toured Pisa, Italy. They took 6 buses.
    How many students were on each bus?

18. Takayoshi, Kevin and Max each had 10 extra pencils. They decided to give the pencils to their classmates. There were 6 other children.
    How many pencils would each child get if the boys divided them evenly?

19. There were 200 people in a restaurant. Each table had 4 people.
    Kevin said there were 52 groups eating in the restaurant. Is he correct? If not, find the correct answer.

20. Rishabh answered 115 math problems on 5 homework assignments. What was the average number of problems on each assignment?

21. Ouri has 2,000 well-packaged cookies. He plans to eat 27 cookies a week. How long will the cookies last? Will there be any left?

22. The detectives solved 21 mysteries in seven days. How many mysteries did they solve each day?

Part Time

1   Ben gets 600 apples each week to feed his horses. He has 20 horses.
Each horse would get how many apples?

2.   There are 60 Gummi Bears and 12 children. How many should each child get if they are divided evenly?

3.   Mark drove his Porsche 105 miles a week. How far did he drive each day? Note: He works 7 days a week! Poor guy!

4.   The nose of the Statue of Liberty is 54 inches in length. Give the length in feet and inches. Remember there are 12 inches in a foot.

5.   Allison answered a total of 115 problems on 5 homework assignments. What was the average number of problems on each assignment?

6.   Mrs. Slane baked 110 cookies. If there are 22 people who work for GTE, how many cookies should each person get?

7.   The trip from Tampa, Florida to Washington, DC is 1,231 miles. How many driving hours will it take if Harold drives at 65 miles per hour?

8.   The cruise ship is 1,236 feet long. How many yards is this?
Remember: 1 yard = 3 feet

9.   Aleksi is going to decorate cars for the parade. He needs 420 meters of crepe paper. If each roll has 30 meters of crepe paper, how many rolls will he need?

10. Tom has a stamp album with 650 stamps in it. The album has 26 pages with the same number of stamps on each page. How many stamps are on each page?

11. A group of 12 students read a total of 156 books. Each student read the same number of books. How many books did each student read?

12. In the telephone book, there are 6,240 names that begin with the letter B.
There are 20 pages in this section. Approximately how many names are on each page?

Just Average

1. The Porsche dealership sold 470 cars, 530 cars, 62 cars, 560 cars, 460 cars and 480 cars. What was the average number of cars sold during the first six months of the year?

2. A student took 6 science tests. She scored 60%, 62%, 64%, 68%, 98% and 99%. What was her average score?

3. Ben had 450 pages to read, Scott had 30 and Rudolph had 300 pages to read. How many pages had to be read?
   What was the average number of pages that had to be read?

4. The art teacher purchased 46 red pencils, 44 orange pencils, 42 yellow pencils and 38 green pencils. What was the average number of pencils that the art teacher purchased?

5. A boy ate 18 chocolates on Monday, 16 on Tuesday, 21 on Wednesday, 15 on Thursday and 10 on Friday. How many chocolates did he eat? What was the average number he ate per day?

6. Jolie spent $400 on a CD player, $50 for a Nintendo game and $82 on a leather jacket. How much did Jolie spend?
   What was the average cost of her purchases?

7. Carlos played 90% of his notes correctly on Monday.
   He played 98% of his notes correctly on Tuesday.
   What was his average?

8. Stephan jet-skied 24 minutes in the morning, 36 minutes in the afternoon and 47 minutes in the evening. How many minutes did he ski? What was the average time he skied?

9. Find the average of 420 kg, 384 kg and 243 kg.

10. Quentin bought five students an ice cream cone. The students had a 3 scoop, a 4 scoop, a 5 scoop, a 6 scoop and a 7 scoop cone.
    What was the average number of scoops?

What Do You Mean

1. Aleksi is 50 years old. Tom is 20 and so is Joe. What is the average age?

2. A car went 31.25 mph. A scooter went 25.63 mph, and a race car went 100.50 mph. Find the average speed.

3. The monkey ate 10 bananas on Monday, 12 on Tuesday, 21 on Wednesday and 34 on Thursday. Find the sum. Find the average.

4. Phillip took three spelling tests. He made a 90%, a 100% and a 50%. What is his test average?

5. In four days Tanya read 42 pages, 46 pages, 35 pages and 57 pages. What was the average number of pages she read each day?

6. Aurelie bought her five friends hotdogs at the game. She made 5 trips. She bought 1, 3, 5, 7 and 9 hotdogs. What was the average per trip?

7. Chris must read 48, 41, 6 and 7 pages for science class this week. Find the total. Find the average number of pages per day.

8. Thomas ate 680 calories for breakfast, 240 for snack, 675 for lunch, 655 for dinner and another 210 before bedtime. How many calories did Tom eat during the day? What was the average number of calories he ate during the day?

9. The boy played 3 games of golf. His scores were 65, 73 and 68. Find his average. Round the number up to the nearest whole number.

10. Five girls swam across the stream. What was the average time? Times: 91 seconds, 78, 86, 72 and 36 seconds

11. Terryck, Tristan and Terence made cookies. They were supposed to put an average of 35 cookies in 4 cookie tins. The tins had 27, 29 and 31 cookies in each. How many must go in the 4th tin?

12. Find the average of 24, 36 and 48.

I Get the Point

1. Mark ran 2.75 miles. Round this number to the nearest tenth.

2. Paul's new car gets 26.925 miles per gallon on the highway. Round 26.925 to the nearest whole number.

3. Steven drove 540.9 miles on Monday, 658.5 miles on Tuesday and 733.4 miles on Wednesday. How far did he drive in all?

4. Calin bought a toy car for $12.45. How much change did he get if he gave the cashier $20.00?

5. Sara's car traveled 313.5 miles on 11 gallons of gas. Her car traveled an average of how many miles per gallon?

6. Harold needs 14 steaks for a barbeque. Each steak will cost $6.25. How much will Harold spend on steaks?

7. Jeanette and Lee took 254 pictures on their trip to Europe. They paid $73.66 to get them all developed. What was the cost per picture?

8. Dale spent $3.25 on a cheeseburger, $1.10 on fries and $2.85 on a chocolate shake. How much did he spend on his meal?

9. A watermelon is $.23 per pound. How much will a 16 pound watermelon cost?

10. A student bought plain pencils at a cost of 5 for $.25. She painted designs on the pencils and sold them for 5 for $.50. How many pencils did she sell to make a $2.50 profit?

11. Michael bought 4 rolls of film for $15.60. Debbie bought 5 rolls of film for $16.10.
    a) How much did Michael pay per roll?
    b) How much did Debbie pay per roll?
    c) Who got the better deal? Explain your answer.

Fractions . . . A Part of the Solution

1. Yushi had 5 cookies on his plate. His sister ate 2 2/3 of them.
    How much was left?

2. Bruce received a bill for $24.80. It was 1/4 more than he expected!
    What amount did he expect?

3. Hana ate 3 3/8 of her pizza. Her dad ate 4 1/3 of his. How much more did her dad eat?

4. Twin fractions were born. One weighed 6 1/4 pounds. The other weighed 25/4 pounds.
    Did they weigh the same amount?

5. Kumiko heard that about 66% of the people lost power to their homes. Write this
    percentage as a reduced fraction.

6. William and Brenden went to a baseball game. The pitcher struck out 2/5 of the batters.
    Make three equivalent fractions.
    2/5 =

7. Stephanie's doctor told her to take 1/2 of 1/8 tsp. of medicine.
    What is 1/2 of 1/8?

8. Kiersten's mom made 3 3/4 cups of oatmeal. She needs to divide it evenly among 5
    bowls. How much should each bowl have?

9. Calin had 130 books in his room. His puppy chewed on 2/10 of them before being
    caught with her paws and jaws on the books!
    Find 2/10 of 130.

10. A piece of property has 64 pine trees on it. The owner needs to trim 1/4 of them. How
    many trees need trimming?

11. A city parking lot has 430 vehicles parked in it. Approximately 3/5 of the vehicles are
    SUV's. How many are not SUV's?

Fantastic Fractions

1. Yushi had 12 cookies. His friend ate 1 7/10 of them. How many did Yushi have left?

2. Allyse made 5 cakes for the party. After the party there were 2 3/5 left. How much cake was eaten?

3. Kana had a cake at her house. Her mom ate 2/8, and her dad ate 3/8.
   How much cake was eaten? How much cake was left?

4. At Jonathon's class party, 2 5/10 of the cheese pizza and 8 2/10 of the mushroom pizza were already gone. How much pizza had been eaten so far?

5. It took Travis 4 5/12 eggs to make his cake right. It took Michael 9 5/12 eggs to make his cake the way he wanted it! How many eggs did the boys use in all?

6. The glass of cold milk was 5/8 full. A girl drank 3/8 of it before the phone rang. What fraction of milk remained in the glass?

7. The ISS Orchestra practiced 6 of 18 concertos. What fraction did the group practice?

8. The teacher ordered 22 small pizzas. The students ate 19 2/3 of them.
   How much was left?

9. Michael's chameleon was 12 3/4 inches long. The body was 6 1/4 inches long. How long was his tail?

10. Alexsi went to the mall with $24.00. He spent 5/6 of his money in the video store. How much money did he spend? How much was left?
    Draw a picture to illustrate the fraction 5/6.

11. Twenty-four of the three dozen bicyclists rode mountain bikes. What fraction of the bikers did <u>not</u> ride mountain bikes?

12. Kunal earned $3.60. He gave 3/8 of it to charity. How much did he give to a worthy cause?

13. At school, 12 of the 40 students in the class drink milk. What fraction drink milk? What fraction of the students do not drink milk?

14. One fourth of the instruments are wind instruments. Write five equivalent fractions!

15. Christopher's horse ran 11/6 kilometers. Kate's horse ran 12/8 km.
    Which horse ran the greatest distance?

16. Dale works 21/2 hours, and he plays 43/4 hours each day. Does he spend more time working or playing?

17. Help Lauren and Andrew double the cookie recipe!

    1 cup sugar
    2/3 cups butter
    2 eggs
    1 1/2 cups flour
    3/4 tsp. vanilla

18. Miss Price had to add 3/4, 6/8 and 9/12. Help her!

19. The Police Department was looking for 5 fractions equivalent to 2/7.
    What are some of the possibilities?

20. Mom and Dad Fraction had a baby. They wanted to name it 80/105.
    The nurse shook her head, and she said it was a hard name to remember.
    Help Mom and Dad Fraction simplify the name.

21. Aya saw 12 muffins in a pan. Four were blueberry. What fraction of the muffins were <u>not</u> blueberry?

22. Nina had a pan of lasagna. She cut it into 20 equal pieces. Terrence ate 8 pieces. What fraction of the lasagna did Terrence eat? Reduce the fraction.

Let's Have a Piece

1. At Jil's birthday party 5/10 of her cake was served to her friends.
    Another 3/10 was enjoyed by her family. What fraction of her cake was eaten? Reduce the fraction.

2. Jon ran 3/4 mile in 9 minutes. James ran 5/9 mile in the same time.
    Who ran the farthest? Draw a picture.

3. Jessica rode her horse around a 1/3 mile track a total of 7 times.
    How many miles did she ride?

4. On Wednesday, 10/20 students ordered the fried chicken. Another 6/20 ordered hamburgers. What fraction of the students ordered lunch? Can you give the percent too?

5. Anton added 7 1/3 cups of strawberries to the ice cream mixture.
    Then he added 5 1/3 cups of soft bananas. How many cups of fruit did he add to his homemade ice cream?

6. On Friday morning, 2/3 of Moyuru's classmates put blackberries on their cereal. If there are 27 kids in his class, how many put blackberries on their cereal?

7. Diane's locker combination is 3 3/5 + 2 2/3 + 2 1/12.
    Find the sum of the fractions.

8. The clerk had 3/4 kg. of nuts. He ate 1/8 of them. How much was left?

9. Phillip needs to make 25 stars for the scenery. He has finished 3/5 of the stars. How many stars has he finished?

10. A person ate 4 3/4 pieces of cake. Another person ate 6 1/3 pieces!
    Find the sum. Find the difference.

11. Hayley and Jennie read that 2/5 of the 30 players in the game had never played soccer before. How many had never played soccer before?

12. The principal said that 3/5 of the 50 participants were girls.
    How many participants were girls? How many were boys?

13. Jeff and Kunal were very hungry! Kunal ate 3 1/8 pizza. Jeff ate 5 1/2 pizza. How much pizza did they eat?

14. Danielle had a ruler. It broke into 2 pieces. One piece was 5 1/4 inches long. How long was the other piece?

15. Hannah decided to make some cookies. The recipe asks for 5/8 cup of orange juice and 1/4 cup of lemon juice. How much liquid does she need?

16. The cook had 6 3/8 chickens. He served 5 2/4 of them. How much was left?

17. Many mammals sleep for long periods. Lions can sleep up to 20 hours a day! What fraction of the day can lions sleep? Reduce this fraction.

18. William thinks that 5/6 of 72 is 12. Is he correct?

19. Joe brought 5 1/2 cakes to the picnic. He could not believe that the people had only eaten half. How much did the people eat?

20. A mom figured out that she spent 4/24 hours of her day in the kitchen. What fraction of the day is mom doing something else? Reduce the fraction.

21. Draw figures showing the equivalent fractions 7/8 and 14/16. Then show the next equivalent fraction.

Measurement Matters

1. Scott and Erin built a table that would seat 24 people.
   The table was 22 feet long and 4 feet wide. What was the perimeter of the table? What was the area of the table?

2. Five pieces of string, each measuring 8 inches, were cut from a roll 6 feet long. What length of string was left?

3. A boy saw on a map where the scale was 5 cm = 1 km.
   He saw where the distance from the hotel to the beach was 35 cm.
   How far away is the beach?

4. The dog chased the cat for 200 meters! Convert meters to centimeters by multiplying 200 x 100.

5. The driveway measured 20 feet by 50 feet. Find the perimeter and the area of the driveway.

6. The landlord told the tenant that the room is 12 feet long, and she also said the area of the room is 144 ft. squared. How wide is the room?

7. The diameter of Cyrille's bicycle tire is 24 inches. What is the circumference?

8. The math teacher drew a circle with a 5-inch radius. What is the circumference?

9. Aleksi saw a huge camphor tree that was 63 feet tall!
   Convert 63 feet to yards. Convert 63 feet to inches.

10. Monday's temperature started at 16 F. It dropped 3 F, rose 21 F, dropped 6 F, and then it rose another 4 F before stabilizing. What was the ending temperature?

11. The space shuttle is worked on inside a building that is 1, 136 feet tall. Convert this to yards.

12. The perimeter of a square is 48 feet. How long is each side?

13. Iku's dad built a rectangular deck. The width of the deck is 14 feet. The perimeter equals 68 feet. The area equals 280 feet squared. Find the dimensions of the deck.

14. The basket has a radius of 12 inches.
    a) What is the diameter?
    b) What is the circumference?

15. The baker said a cake with a diameter of 9 inches and a circumference of _____ inches would feed 8 people. We can predict a cake with an 18 inch diameter and a circumference of _____ inches would feed approximately _____ people!

16. Ian, Dave and George intend to build a storage shed. The shed will be 14 meters by 28 meters. Find the perimeter and the area.

17. A developer bought a piece of property that had an overall area of 7,500 sq. meters. Can he build a hotel 56 meters by 78 meters?

18. Alessandra read that her dorm room had an area of 300 sq. feet.
    Which measurements would be the <u>most</u> practical?

19. Dina ate a square pizza. Each side measured 6 inches. Find the perimeter and the area of her pizza.

20. A Christmas tree was 2 meters and 36 cm tall. A man had to cut off 47cm in order for it to fit in his house. What was the height of the tree after the man cut some off?

21. The freight car weighs 5.5 tons! Convert this to pounds.
    (Hint: 2,000 pounds = 1 ton)

Undercover

1. I am 70 greater than the product of 42 and 16. Who am I?

2. I am 49 less than the product of 232 and 34. Who am I?

3. I am the answer when 82 is multiplied by the sum of 7 and 8. Who am I?

4. Who are we? Our sum is 13, and our product is 40.

5. Our sum is 11, and our product is 30. Who are we?

6. Our product is 64, and our sum is 20. Who are we?

7. The sum of the two numbers is 136. The difference is 62, and the product is 3,663. One number is 99. The other one is _____.

8. Cory was upset because there were 5 people on his team instead of 4C =48! C = _____

9. Detectives were looking for two suspects, but they did not know their names. The sum of the numbers is 26, and the product of the same two numbers is 168. What numbers are the detectives looking for?

10. Our sum is 23, and our product is 102. Who are we?

11. The bank teller had to figure out the missing number in order to open the bank safe. Help him to find the missing number.
    $6x + 7 = 61$ x = _____

12. Rebecca told her mom she got 3 x 2 x 4 x 2 x 2 on her math test. What was her percentage score?

13. Matt found ½ of a treasure map on the beach. In order to find the coordinates for the buried treasure he must find the mystery number.
    When the number is added to itself, the answer is 16. When the number is multiplied by itself, the answer is 64. What is it?

Solve It

1. The product of two numbers is 24. The sum of the numbers is 11.
    What are the two numbers?

2. Two of the suspects refused to talk to the detectives. The product of their numbers is 45.
    The sum of their numbers is 14. Who are they?

3. Greg is trying to solve a mystery. Help him out! Two of the suspects were too busy to talk
    to the detectives. The sum of their numbers is 10.
    The product of their numbers is 24. Who are they?

4. The thieves were caught with the diamonds. The product of their numbers is 144. The
    sum of their numbers is 25. Who are they?

5. Two of the team members are cousins. The product of their numbers is 48. The sum of
    their numbers is 14. Who are they?

6. Two numbers were in the garden. The product of the numbers is 36.
    The sum of the numbers is 13. Who are they?

7. Miki called the detectives because his numbers were missing. He told the detectives the
    sum of the numbers was 42. The product was 392.
    What were the numbers?

8. The product of the two numbers is 56. The sum is 15. What are the numbers?

9. Harold had a box of 40 golf balls. Two disappeared. Which two disappeared if the sum
    of the numbers is 39, and the product of the numbers is 108?

10. Sara and Monica ate a whole watermelon. Sara had the sum of 33 seeds. Monica had the
    product of 252 seeds. What were the two numbers that gave the girls these seeds?

11. _____ + _____ = 29 mpg/town _____ X _____ = 210 mpg/highway

Popular Percentages

1. Twenty-five percent of the students play an organized sport.
   There are 640 students. How many play an organized sport?

2. Eighty percent of the 50 answers on the science test are correct.
   Write 80% as a reduced fraction. Find the number of correct answers on the test.

3. There are 42,500 people who voted in the election. Seventy percent voted yes for building a new school. How many voted for the new school? How many voted against building a new school?

4. The state income tax is 7%. How much tax would a person pay if their income is $45,000?

5. Roy spent $12.95 on a new soccer ball. He had to pay a 4% sales tax.
   How much sales tax did Roy pay? Find the total cost of the ball.

6. Ouri took a history quiz. He got 14 out of 20 correct.
   What percentage did he earn on his quiz?

7. Calin saw that the scooters were 30% off. The scooter he wanted was marked $56.00.
   How much should Calin save? What will the sale price be?

8. Ms. Kinney took 84 cookies to the party. People ate 98% of them!
   How many cookies were eaten? How many cookies were left?

9. The Easter Bunny got 12/50 test questions correct on his Egg Test.
   Find the percentage he got correct.

10. Liam made 18/24 goals. Reduce this fraction.
    What percentage of the goals did he make?

11. There are 30 kids in the group. Thirty percent earned an A on their science test. How many earned an A?

12. The garden has 3,600 flowers, and 64% of them have an insect on them. How many flowers have an insect on them?

13. George drove 1,700 miles in two days! He drove 55% the first day, and he drove 45% the second day. He drove _____ miles the first day, and he drove _____ the second day.

14. Mrs. Delgado said, "It seems like Don thinks about motorcycles 25% of 24 hours!" How much does Don think about motorcycles?

15. A person talked 90% of the 240 minute flight. How long did the person talk?

16. Mike missed 5% of the school year because he had the flu. There are 180 school days. How many days of school did Mike miss?

17. Randy got a cool-looking hair cut. He paid $24.95 for the cut, and he gave the barber a 20% tip. How much did Randy spend?

18. The spokesman for the health department said, "We expect 15% of the 100 days of summer to be over 95 F!" Reduce this fraction.

19. The teacher was very frustrated! Out of 120 students, about 20% of them did not do their homework! How many students did not do their homework?

20. Approximately 16/80 of the flights were delayed. What percentage of flights is this?

21. There are 200 houses in a neighborhood. About 70% have a 3-car garage. How many houses have a 3-car garage?

22. There are 12 Asian elephants at the zoo. Eight of them are in the water. Write 8/12 as a percentage.

23. Twelve out of fifteen new businesses in town employ more than five people. Find the equivalent percentage.

A Part of It

1. Mark ate 75% of the 360 pieces of spaghetti. He ate _____ pieces.

2. Lee applied to 20 colleges. He was accepted at 60% of them.
    He was accepted at _____, and he was rejected by _____.

3. A doll smiles 80% of a day. How many minutes does the doll smile?

4. Donnie answered 55/70 of his science questions correct.
    Find his percentage score.

5. Steven earned $277.00 building a shed for his neighbor. He had to give 45% of it to the bank to repay a loan. How much would Steven have left?

6. A man won $500.00 in a drawing. He spent 25% of it on new clothes, and he saved 75% of it in his savings account. How much did the man spend on clothes?

7. A family is out to dinner. The total bill is $27.50.
    How much should a 15% tip be?

8. Tom was able to spell 30/35 of his vocabulary words.
    Find his percentage.

9. The woman sold $436.00 worth of supplies. She earned a 15% commission on her sales. How much did she earn?

10. The teacher has graded 25% of 44 papers. How many papers has the teacher graded? How many more are left to grade?

11. The cookie plant has to toss out 2% of their cookies because they are defective. If the plant makes 10,000 cookies each day, how many cookies do they toss out a day?

12. Mrs. Cook left 60 cookies on the kitchen counter. Her dog ate 5% of them. How many cookies did the dog eat?

It's About Time

1. Eric has an appointment in 2 hours and 30 minutes. What time is his appointment if it is 8:40 AM now?

2. Ouri practices guitar for 3/4 of an hour every day. How many minutes does he practice each day? How long does he practice in a week?

3. Emily's phone bill showed that she talked on the phone for 25 minutes. The call started at 4:12 PM. What time did the call end?

4. Iku's flight left Stuttgart at 8:25 AM. It arrived in London at 10:40 AM. How long was her flight?

5. Phillip is going to Strasbourg, France. He will leave Stuttgart, Germany at 10:15 AM and arrive at 12:07 PM. How long is the train trip?

6. The performance for Mr. Garvey began at 7:45 PM, and it ended at 10:25 PM. How long was the performance?

7. Travis, Michael, Jeffrey and James went to a movie. It lasted 105 minutes. If it started at 2:00 PM, at what time did it end?

8. Cyrille wanted to eat Mexican for dinner. He parked his red Porsche in the parking lot. If the parking garage charges $1.50 per half hour, what is the cost of parking a car from 6:15 PM until 10:45 PM?

9. Tim went to the batting cage at 10:45 AM. He finally got tired at 11:52 AM. How long did Tim practice?

10. Seda and Federica stayed a total of 53 hours at the Grand Canyon. How many days and extra hours was that in all?

11. Brendan spends 2 hours and 15 minutes doing homework each night. Convert this into seconds.

12. Sara slept from 7:40 PM until 6:15 AM. How long did she sleep?

Time Out

1. The train ride was 15 hours long. Mark slept 65% of it. How long did Mark sleep? Round your answer to the nearest hour.

2. Mr. Wilkes woke up at 7:05 AM, and he went to sleep at 9:30 PM. How long was Mr. Wilkes awake?

3. Harold left St. Louis at 7:00 AM, and he arrived in Texas at 12:21 PM. How long was his travel time?

4. Jeanette wanted to call her son in Portugal. Portugal is 5 hours ahead of Florida. If it is 10:30 PM in Florida, what time is it in Portugal?

5. Maya feeds her baby every 3 hours. She fed it at 11:00 AM. List the next five feeding times.

6. Jessica has a major English paper due tomorrow morning! She is planning on working on it from 6:35 PM until 11:15 PM. How long will Jessica spend working on her paper?

7. Galia's school day is from 7:30 AM until 2:45 PM. How long is her school day?

8. Tawna's train left Stuttgart at 7:11 AM, and it arrived in Brussels at 12:07 PM. How long was Tawna's train ride?

9. Convert 5 hours and 23 minutes to minutes.

10. Place the following in order from the shortest to the longest.
    3,000 minutes   49 hours   2 days & 4 hours

11. Finish the pattern: 4:45 PM 5:25 PM 6:05 PM _____

12. Lee looked at a clock. It was 8:48 AM. What time will it be in 4 hours and 20 minutes?

13. Paul had the hiccups. He hiccupped every 8 minutes. Finish the pattern.
    6:07 PM 6:15 _____ _____ _____ _____ PM

14. Meg worked on her book a total of 63 hours over 14 days. She worked the same time each day. How long did she work each day?

15. The girls at the sleepover slept from 10:56 PM until 7:30 AM.
    How long did the girls sleep?

16. Dale spent 2 hours and 15 minutes practicing baseball. Convert this to minutes. Convert this to seconds.

17. Dominick slept 7 hours and 40 minutes. His sister slept 9 hours and 50 minutes. Find the total amount they slept.

18. Jackie left Munich at 7:37 PM. She arrived in Rome at 10:59 AM the next morning. How long was Jackie's train ride?

19. Steven had numerous errands to run. He had two hours. He had to drive 20 minutes each way. If he had 7 errands to do, what is the average time he should allow for each errand?

20. The trucker has to drive 650 miles to his destination. The speed limit is 55 mph on the interstate. His trip will take him almost _____ hours!

21. The Kinney's drove 600 miles in 8 hours. What was their average speed? At this speed, how far can they go in 12 hours?

22. Ed sleeps from 10:30 PM until 5:30 AM each day. How long does Ed sleep in a week? How long does he sleep in a year?

23. It takes 20 minutes to write 15 sentences. At this rate, how long would it take to write 60 sentences?

24. Andre, Greg, Samantha and Kate flew to Atlanta from Germany.
    They left at 11:45 AM and arrived at 9:30 PM German time.
    Atlanta is 6 hours behind Germany. What time did they get to Atlanta?

A Bit More Challenging

1. A Harley Davidson motorcycle rumbles once at 1:00, twice at 2:00, three times at 3:00 and so forth. How many times does it rumble during 24 hours?

2. List at least six different numbers using 3,5, 7 and 9.
   They must be three digit numbers.

3. The sum of Calin's age and his dad's age is 56. Calin's dad is seven times older than Calin. How old is Calin?

4. For dessert Catrina can choose apple, cherry, blackberry or peach pie to eat and milk or juice to drink. How many different combinations can she choose from?

5. A boy is saving to buy a bike that costs $360.00. He has already saved ½ of the money. If he saves $20.00 per week, will he be able to purchase the bike within 3 months?

6. The team's average score for three basketball games is 33 points.
   They scored 27 and 39 in the first two games. What score did they have in the third game?

7. Write the next number. Explain.
   a) 7, 15, 22, 30, 37, 45, _____
   b) 110, 100, 80, 50, _____

8. Which hit the ground first? Explain your answer.
   500 lbs. of cotton   500 lbs. of jelly beans   500 lbs. of potatoes

9. Citizens in the United States are eligible to vote at age 18. Dave was born in 1964. Circle the elections he could have voted in.
   1972   1976   1980   1984   1988   1992   1996   2000   2004   2008

10. The teacher added an even number and an odd number.
    Would the sum be an odd or an even number?

11. Multiply the number of letters in the alphabet by the number of planets. What is the product? Can you list the 8 planets in order from the sun?

12. Mark, Paul, Gail, Steven and Harold are all different ages.
    Harold is the oldest, and Steven is the youngest. Paul is between Mark and Gail. Mark is the second oldest. List the names of the five people, from oldest to youngest.

13. Can you predict if 858 is evenly divisible by three? If so, how?
    (Hint: Is there a rule about dividing by three?)

14. A bag of corn has 12 ears in it. A bag of tomatoes has 9 in it.
    What is the fewest number of bags you would have to buy to have exactly the same number of vegetables?
    Show your work.

15. There are a total of 15 animals on a farm. Horses and ducks live on the farm. There are a total of 42 legs. How many horses and ducks live on the farm?

16. The American flag has 50 stars on it. List all the factors of 50.

17. Nicole had a dog. It had 10 puppies. Nicole sold three, gave away two, and she kept the rest. How many <u>dogs</u> does she have left?

18. Travis rented a trailer to drive to Texas. It was 8 feet long and 5 feet wide. He loaded the trailer with 1 ft. x 1 ft. x 1 ft. boxes to a height of 3 feet. How many boxes did he load?

19. The temperature was 16 F at 5:00 PM. It was – 17 F at 10:00 PM.
    Find the difference in temperatures.

We've Got Problems

1. Phillip bought 6 pairs of earrings for his sister. Each pair cost $3.89. How much did he spend on the earrings?

2. Elsie drove a total of 489 minutes to get to her destination.
   Convert this to hours and minutes.

3. Kevin was a millionaire. He had $2,345,987.00 in his account.
   He spent $944,999.99 on a new house. How much was left in his account after purchasing the house?

4. The local radio station played the holiday song 5 times on Monday.
   The song was 2 minutes and 38 seconds long. Find the total time the song played on Monday.

5. There are 27 actors in a play. Each gets paid only $39.52 a day.
   The play runs for 14 days. How much will the production company pay in salaries?

6. A girl can read 20 pages in an hour. At this rate, how many pages can she read in 40 hours?

7. Find the Greatest Common Factor (GCF) of 56 & 14.

8. Lucy's mom took her shopping for her 13th birthday. Lucy bought a shirt for $8.95, a pair of shoes for $ 31.75 and a new purse for $25.00. How much money was spent?

9. The Easter Bunny discovered that some of his eggs were missing!
   He started out with 892, and he ended up with 278. How many eggs were missing?

10. A girl sold 36 boxes of cookies. Her friend sold 7 times that many.
    How many boxes of cookies did the friend sell? How many boxes of cookies did they sell together?

11. Four boys entered a pie-eating contest. They ate 3/4, 2/4, 1/3 and 2/3 of their personal pie. Find the sum!

12. Steven got 16/20 of his history questions correct. Find his percentage.

13. Emma can travel 37 km on a liter of gas. How much gas would she need to travel 1,110 kilometers?

14. Ceyda was on School Time, an educational show for kids! She was asked to name the mnemonic device for remembering the order of operations. Can you help her? Please _____ _____ dear Aunt _____.

15. Haley and Nick wanted a pizza, but they did not know the phone number. Nick's dad said to find the square roots for the numbers.
Pizza Palace: 9, 16, 25 – 49, 100, 64

16. Taylor wants to buy her mom a gift that costs $102.56. She only has $53.68. Her dad might lend her $ _____ so she could buy it.

17. Sierra found 15% of the 60 eggs. How many did she find?

18. The teacher had the test locked away in his desk. He forgot his combination. Help him remember the 3rd number.
    2 7/8 + 5 3/4 =

19. Mrs. Frosch baked 6 dozen cookies. She divided them evenly among 4 families. How many cookies did each family get?

20. Varun bought 15 bags of marshmallows. Each bag had 60 in it.
How many marshmallows did he buy?

21. There were 15 sheets of cookies. Each cookie sheet had 15 cookies on it. How many cookies were baked?

22. Savion spent $29.75 on 5 of the same thing. How much was each?

23. Ryan left school at 3:10 PM and returned at 5:37 PM. How long was he gone?

A Little Bit of Everything

1. Anton walks 4 blocks in 9 minutes. At this speed, how many minutes does it take him to walk 16 blocks?

2. Mrs. Brown was planning on making Snickerdoodles for her daughter's bake sale. She needs to triple the recipe. Help her.

   2 1/2 cups flour
   2 tsp. cream of tarter
   1 tsp. baking soda
   1/2 tsp. salt
   1 cup Crisco
   1 1/4 cups sugar
   2 eggs
   1 tsp. vanilla
   2 TB sugar
   1 tsp. each nutmeg and cinnamon

3. A boy reads 29 pages in 1 hour. At this rate, it will take _____ hours to read a 1,653 page book.

4. An outdoor theater in Italy can hold 490 people. Each row has 35 seats in it. How many rows are there?

5. Calin read 56 books. Each book had 4,149 words. Find the product.

6. The PTA has $2005.26. It wants to divide it evenly among three projects. How much will each project receive?

7. A man played 3 games of golf. His scores were 65, 73 and 68.
   Find his average score.

8. Mr. Line's phone number is 362-213-1483. Add all the digits to find the sum. Multiply all the digits to find the product.

9. Travis talked to Billy Bob for 45.5 minutes. It cost him $.12 a minute.
   How much does Travis owe the phone company?

10. A student found $250.00. Factor 250 into prime numbers.

11. There are 91 days in the 1st semester of school. School begins at 8:30 AM and it ends at 3:00 PM. A student has been in school _____ hours during the 1st semester!

12. (A-Z) (5 vowels) =

13. (A-Z) / (5 vowels) =

14. One candidate received 205,209 votes. Another candidate received 137,785 votes. Find the sum. Find the difference.

15. In 1996, President Clinton won against Bob Dole with 379 electoral votes. Find the percentage each received.

    Clinton: 379/538   Dole: 159/538

16. 3,410,511 – 2,669,374 =

17. An antique car is 96 years old. Factor 96 into prime numbers.

18. A student bought 3 school T-shirts. Each shirt cost $8.50.
    How much did the student spend on T-shirts?

19. A bicyclist rides 207 meters in one minute. How far can she ride in 19 minutes?

20. Find the two mystery numbers! The sum of the digits is 18. The product of the digits is 72. What are the two mystery numbers?

21. Fifteen percent of the cars in the parking lot were foreign brands.
    There were 40 cars in the lot. How many were foreign brands?

22. A person ate 2,500 calories yesterday. She burned off 12% of them by taking a bike ride. How many calories did she burn off by exercising?

23. Steven took a bite out of 35% of 20 doughnuts. How many whole doughnuts were left?

Mixing it Up

1. Aleksi is applying for a job. He has to answer these questions correctly. What should his answers be? a) Find 25% of 48. b) What is 8% of $15.00? c) Find 7% of $8.98, and round the answer to the nearest cent.

2. The city parking garage charges $1.50 an hour. If you parked there from 11:15 AM – 2:45 PM, how much would you pay?

3. Lillian wants to pay off her new Harley Davidson within 12 months. It costs $14,500.00. How much will she have to pay each month?

4. Kumiko bought five pizzas for $23.75. Her friend bought 7 pizzas for $33.95.
   a) How much did Kumiko pay per pizza?
   b) How much did the friend pay per pizza?
   c) Find the average price per pizza.

5. Felix collected 111 milk jugs. Three people gave him the same number of jugs. How many jugs did he get from each person?

6. Ben rode his bike 3 days in a row. He rode 44 minutes Friday, 49 minutes Saturday and 75 minutes on Sunday. Find the average time he rode.

7. Eight peaches can be purchased for $3.84. How much does each peach cost? How much would 10 peaches cost?

8. Courtney bought 4 apple trees for $16.95 each, 2 peach trees for $18.95 each, and she bought pumpkin seeds for $3.95.
   How much did Courtney spend?

9. A man can pick 6 blackberries every 30 seconds. At this rate, how many blackberries can he pick in 20 minutes?

10. The ratio of girls to boys at camp is 7 to 5. If there are 20 boys, how many girls are there?

11. Danielle can type 40 words a minute. At this rate, how many words can she type in 20 minutes?

12. Eric earned $68.00 for 8 hours of work. How much should he earn working a 40 hour week?

13. The radius of a circle is 12 centimeters. What is the diameter?
    Find the circumference.   (Hint: C = 3.14 x D)

14. The art teacher can buy 14 packs of clay for $63.00. How much will the art teacher spend on 20 packs of clay?

15. Alba got 7/8 questions correct on her quiz. Find her percentage.

16. Mike caught 8/12 throws during the football game. Find his percentage.

17. What is the probability of drawing a vowel (a,e,i,o,u) out of the alphabet? Can this fraction be reduced?

18. Mr. Garvey's science lab is 35 feet long and 25 feet wide.
    Find the perimeter and the area of his lab.

19. The board in the locker room has an area of 54 sq. feet.
    Find the most practical measurements for a board.

20. Find the average of 38, 42, 44 and 46.

21. The average of 8, 16, 24 and _____ is 20!

22. The travel agent will order train tickets for 17 students.
    Each ticket is $48.52. How much will the travel agent collect from the customer?

23. Queen Elizabeth came to the throne in 1952. She is still the Queen of England. How long has she reigned so far?

Around the House

1. The Kent family ordered 3 large pizzas. Each was cut into 8 pieces.
   The family ate 80% of the pizza. Approximately how many slices did they eat?

2. Dad wants a new power tool. The price is $56.90. He can get 40% off the price if he pays cash. Calculate his savings.

3. Hannah has a bag of marbles. There are eight red marbles, 10 blue marbles and 2 green marbles. What is the probability of Hannah picking a green marble?

4. The local newspaper said the high temperature would be 92 F, and the low temperature would be 71 F. Find the sum, difference, and the product of the two temperatures.

5. Mom's book is 840 pages long. Factor 840 into prime numbers.

6. Will had coupons for the following amounts:
   $.40 $.75 $.50 $.25 $.40
      a) Find the mean (average)
      b) Find the median (middle number when the numbers are in order)
      c) Find the mode (number that occurs must often)

7. Brenden, Michael, Courtney and Karl earned $35.00 for cleaning the yard. If they divide the money evenly, how much will each person receive?

8. Amy found 82 quarters in her piggy bank. How much money did she find?

9. Elizabeth heard that 1/5 of the 300 troops were returning tomorrow.
   How many troops are returning tomorrow?

10. Bill left his house at 6:45 AM, and he returned at 5:58 PM.
    How long was Bill away from the house?

11. Faye needs 8 1/4 yards of material to make new curtains.
    The roll of cloth has 10 2/3 yards on it. How much extra cloth will Faye have?

12. Dave loves making model cars! He wants to make 8 cars.
    Each car has 64 pieces. How many pieces are there in 8 cars?

13. Farmer Brown had 28 hens. Each hen laid 3 eggs each day.
    How many eggs did he get in a week?

14. Maeve had 3 2/3 pizzas. Yannick had 5 5/9 pizzas. Find the sum.

15. Ms. Price left 19 1/2 doughnuts in her kitchen. When she returned, only 7 1/4 remained!
    How many had disappeared?

16. Sung Min bought 15 pounds of peaches for $.89 per pound.
    How much did Sung Min spend on peaches?

17. Alexander felt ill. He went to sleep at 3:28 PM, and he woke up at 5:14 AM. How long
    did he sleep?

18. Brett is building a balcony. He wants to convert 39 feet to yards.
    Help him.

19. The family is playing a game of cards. What is the probability of drawing a red queen
    from a normal deck of 52 cards?

20. A girl can stuff 25 envelopes in 5 minutes. At this rate, how many envelopes can she stuff
    in 60 minutes?

21. A gallon of gas cost $3.06. How much will dad spend to fill up his 5 gallon lawnmower?

22. The electric bill was $246.80. Mom wants to reduce the bill next month by 20%. How
    much would Mom like to save?

23. Sara bought a 16 ounce package of butter for $1.99.
    She spent approximately $._____ on each ounce.

Back to School

1. Andy bought 3 stretchable book covers for a total of $.99.
    How much was each book cover?

2. Kaitlyn purchased 3 composition books. Each one cost $.66.
    What was the sum of her purchases?

3. Marta couldn't believe the great deal she read about! She could get 2 backpacks for $9.99.
    She only had $6.48. How much more does she need?

4. Angel was leaving for college. Her mom gave her 8 packages of film so she could send
    pictures home. Each package had 24 exposures. How many pictures can Angel take with
    all the film?

5. Lindsay woke up at 6:15 AM. Her bus came at 7:38 AM.
    How long did Lindsay have to get ready for school?

6. The 6th grade homeroom teacher purchased 22 locks. Each lock was $3.69. How much
    did the teacher spend?

7. Mechanical pencils were on sale. Phillip purchased 3 packs for a total of $2.49. How
    much was each pack?

8. Sarah's history teacher told her to buy a package of 6 highlighters.
    She found a package of six that cost $2.64. How much did each highlighter cost?

9. Katy bought tape, glue, a pencil case and a protractor. She spent $7.38. She gave the
    clerk a $10.00 bill. How much change should Katy have gotten back?

10. Four children bought school supplies. Chris bought 5 things, Iku bought 10 things, Adam
    bought 15, and Felix bought only 6 things. Find the average number of purchases.

11. The school bus was 10 feet wide and 30 feet long. Find the perimeter and the area of the
    school bus.

12. Ms. Cunningham told her aide that the new classroom was 300 sq. feet. The width of
    the room is 15 feet. What is the length?

13. Dina's dad bought her a fancy calculator for $54.98. He had to pay a 5% sales tax. Find the total price for the calculator.

14. The football player was told to report to practice at exactly 2:15 PM. He sees that it is 1:47 PM. How long does he have before practice?

15. Carmen has 7 periods a day. Each class lasts 40 minutes. How long is Carmen in class each day?

16. Megan has a 300-pack of index cards. She has already used 50 of them. Approximately what percentage of the cards does she have left?

17. Scott attends college 369 miles away. His sister wants to mail him some cookies. The postman tells her it will take 3 days for her box to arrive at Scott's address. Find the average distance the box travels a day.

18. Ian has a crate that is 11 inches wide, 14 inches long and 11inches high. Find the perimeter, area and volume of Ian's crate.

19. George has to walk 1,320 feet to get to the cafeteria. What fraction of 5,280 feet is this?

20. There will be 12 home games during the football season. Each ticket will cost $3.50. If a student goes to every home game, how much will the student spend?

21. The music teacher is very predictable. She gives a quiz every 4 days! There are 180 school days in a school year. How many quizzes can her students expect during the year?

22. Dionte's zip code at college is 23834. Find the sum of the digits. Find the product of the digits.

23. Three boys are sharing the costs of an apartment. Their rent is $885.78/month. How much will each boy pay per month?

Daily Dose

1. Danielle found an old clock in her mom's trunk. The radius of the clock is 4 cm. Help her find the circumference of the clock.

2. Help Nishitha add 3 1/3 cups of sugar to 2 1/4 cups of sugar.

3. Jolie said, "_____% of the months of the year begin with the letter J."

4. In order for Hannah to enter the party she has to factor 750 into prime numbers. What should her answer be?

5. Jon is 5 1/2 feet tall. He is how many inches tall?

6. Cyrille and Tom said, "The probability of drawing a "heart" from a normal deck of 52 cards is 1/4." Were they correct? Explain.

7. What is the sales tax on a $20.00 purchase if the sales tax rate is 7%?

8. Ouri could get an extra "brownie point" if he could write the prime factorization of 225. What should his answer look like?

9. Aleski and Kunal saw a pile of wood that was stacked 5 ft. wide, 6 ft. high and 10 ft. long. How many cubic feet of wood did they see?

10. After reading page 132, Lillian figured she had read 3/4 of her book. How many pages are in her book?

11. Travis and Jon were judges for a competition. The scores they gave were 9.9, 9.8, 9.6 and 10.0! The highest and the lowest scores were not counted. What was the mean/average of the two middle scores?

12. Mr. Gatley said, "Five pounds of beans will fit into each container." How many containers are needed for 740 pounds of beans?

13. Coco and Maxi developed 5 rolls of film. The machine took 30 seconds to develop 2 rolls of film. How long did it take to develop the five rolls of film?

14. Rebecca saw where 415 blocks came in each unit. If 29,050 blocks were required, how many units had to be obtained?

15. Carlotta wanted to answer this question correctly so she could get a free trip to Disney World. Was she correct? She said, "I can check subtraction by adding. I can check my division by multiplying the quotient and the divisor and adding the remainder."

16. Two girls went to the store. They saw where 24 peaches could be purchased for $9.60. What is the price per peach?

17. Scott wanted to figure out what 78 train trips would cost if 50 trips cost $3150.00. Can you help him?

18. Rudolph and Julius figured that the area in sq. ft. of a room that is 12 feet long and 9 feet wide is 145 squared. Is their calculation correct? If not, find the correct area.

19. A gallon of milk costs $2.80. What is the price per quart?

20. Ben chose to answer the question behind door #3. "Which of these bicycle parts is the best example of the circumference of a wheel?"
    Should he answer spoke, axle or tire?

21. The Post Office can normally process letters at a rate of 2,500 per hour.
    During the holidays, the rate can triple. How many hours would it take to process 60,000 letters during the holiday season?

22. Diane took a taxi to the airport. The taxi charged $1.25 for the first mile and $.95 for each additional mile. What was the cost of her seven mile ride?

23. Victoria ran 4 laps in 5 minutes. How many seconds did it take to run each lap if she ran at a steady pace?

24. Jeff arrived at the train station at noon. His train had left 3 hours and 45 minutes before that! What time did the train leave? Where was the train going? Why was Jeff so late?

Food for Thought

1. Ouri baked 105 bran muffins. He gave each person 5 muffins.
   How many people ate his muffins?

2. Victoria had a bag of M & Ms. There were 96 in the bag. If she divided them equally among three people, how many would each person get?

3. A lady had 3 boxes of chocolate. Each box had 48 pieces.
   How many pieces of chocolate are there?

4. A boy sold 148 candy bars for $.75 each. How much did he earn?

5. A cook bought 6 bags of potatoes. Each bag was $2.72. How much did the cook spend on potatoes?

6. Sara spent $4.50 for ingredients for chocolate chip cookies.
   She sold 50 cookies for $.35 each. How much did Sara collect?
   How much profit did she make?

7. Chelsey found a watermelon that weighed 5 pounds. Her brother found a cantaloupe that weighed 3.5 pounds. Find the sum of the melons. Find the difference between the melons.

8. The average pumpkin weighs 6 pounds. The Great Pumpkin weighs 342 pounds! The Great Pumpkin weighs as much as how many average pumpkins?

9. There are 650 pieces of spaghetti in a 2 pound box. Each piece of spaghetti is 8 inches long. Laid end to end, how many feet would the noodles in a package reach?

10. A father wanted to get the biggest pumpkin he could get.
    Pumpkins cost $.30 per pound. The father only had $5.00 to spend. His pumpkin could weigh as much as _____ pounds!

11. Betty Baker wants to make cupcakes for 150 students.
    Each box of cake mix makes 24 cupcakes. How many boxes of cake mix does Betty Baker need?

12. Twelve cases of water can be purchased for $33.36.
    How much does each case cost? How much would twenty cases cost?

13. Nick's dad gave him $10.00 to go shopping. He purchased bread for $1.19, milk for $1.99, cereal for $2.25 and eggs for $.84. He wanted to buy a candy bar for himself and two friends. Each candy bar was $.69.
    a) How much would three candy bars cost?
    b) How much would Nick spend on non-candy items?
    c) Does Nick have enough to buy the 3 candy bars and the groceries?

14. Felix earned $4.00 for every hour he worked in his mom's vegetable garden. If he earned $36.00, how long did he work?

15. The grandmother was planning on making 100 decorated eggs for the Easter Egg Hunt. How many dozen (12) eggs does she need? (Hint: Remember it is better to have too many, than not enough!)

16. A cup of nuts has approximately 170 times as many calories as a cup of lettuce! The lettuce has 5 calories. How many calories are in a cup of nuts?

17. Doctors suggest drinking 3 8oz. glasses of milk a day. How many ounces would be consumed in a week?

18. Marcie collected $4.50 selling lemonade at $.25 a cup.
    How many cups of lemonade did she sell?

19. There are 320 bits in an ounce of cereal. How many bits are there in a one pound box? (Hint: 1 pound = 16 ounces)

Holiday Story Problems

1. Nishitha threw 48 snowballs. Kate threw 6 times more. How many did Kate throw? How many did the girls throw in all?

2. Each reindeer can carry 70 pounds. There are eight of them. Santa weighs 750 pounds. How many more reindeer are needed to carry Santa?

3. Evan ate 3 cookies on Monday. He ate 4 on Tuesday. If he continued this pattern, how many cookies would he eat in a week?

4. Jon ate 52 pieces of fudge. Michael ate 75. What is the difference?

5. Ali bought 3 dozen cookies to the concert. Joe bought 5 dozen. How many cookies are there in all?

6. There were 1,728 ornaments on Danielle's tree. One third were red. How many of the ornaments were red? Do we know the other colors?

7. Eric is working in the kitchen. He must make 44 cups of hot chocolate. Each cup is supposed to have 3 marshmallows. How many marshmallows will Eric need?

8. The reindeer traveled 710,708 miles on Christmas Eve. What is 1/4 of that number?

9. Santa Claus went to Jackson's house at 1:28 AM. He went to Erin's house at 5:39 AM. How much time elapsed between the two visits?

10. Austin and Dominique watched Santa Claus wrap presents for 5 hours. He wrapped 1,958 the first hour. He wrapped 1,960, 1,962, 1,964 and 1,968 the rest of the time. What was the average numbers of presents wrapped per hour?

11. Carlotta received 650 CDs. Her little brother thought they were frisbies and broke 3/10 of them. How many CDs were broken?

12. Ryon had 16 candy canes, Nadav had 25, David had 11 and Tom had 18. Find the sum. Find the average.

13. Daisuke had $1,038.00 in his bank account. He wanted to spread goodwill so he divided the money evenly among three charities. Each charity would get $ _____ !

14. Shateria and Nina had a roof on their classroom that was 24 meters by 12 meters. Do you think Santa had greater than or less than 144 square meters to land his sleigh on? Find the perimeter and the area of the roof.

15. Nicole wanted to get 30 hats. Each hat cost $15.00. Nicole got 12 hats less than she wanted. How much did her parents spend on hats?

16. Rebecca was having 40 people for dinner, including herself. She wanted to make 5 different pies. Each pie should be sliced into _____ pieces so each person can have 1 piece.

17. Murrell did 49 holiday story problems on the last day of school.
Each problem took 30 seconds to work out. How long did it take?
Murrell took _____ seconds to do the problems or _____ minutes.

18. Brett is going to Texas. There are six people in his family. Each ticket costs $1,362.00. How much will his family pay?

19. Tyler had 200 decorations on his tree. James put 50 candles on the tree.
Ms. Price accidentally knocked over the tree. She broke 4/5 of the decorations. How many decorations were <u>not</u> broken?

20. Travis went snowboarding for three days. On the first day he fell 12 times. On the second he fell 18 times, and on the third he fell 24 times.
Following this pattern, if Travis were to snowboard a fourth day, he would fall _____ times! Find the sum. Find the average.

21. The 6th graders went on a field trip to the Berlin Christmas market.
They left the school at 8:30 AM and traveled for 5 hours to get there.
What time did they arrive in Berlin?

22. Mrs. Pray woke up at 1:36 AM because she heard a thump. If Santa talked until 3:47 AM, ate cookies, drank milk and figured out Rudloph's emotional state of mind, how long was the visit?

It's a Hurricane

1. The hurricane's winds were blowing at 134 mph on Monday. On Tuesday, the winds were only 76 mph. What was the difference?

2. Hurricanes must have winds of at least 74 mph. If the winds are only 56 mph, how much do the winds need to increase to be a hurricane?

3. A town next to the ocean has a population of 5,650 people. Approximately 75% of the people are prepared for a hurricane. How many people are prepared? (Hint: 5,650 x .75)

4. A woman reads that bottled water costs $1.25 a gallon. She needs to buy 12 gallons. How much will she spend?

5. Sara owns a horse farm. She has 56 horses that she needs to evacuate to a safer area. Each trailer that she owns can carry 8 horses. How many trailers does she need?

6. The weather forecaster said the hurricane could hit with speeds of __ __ __ mph! Use the clue to answer the question.
   Clue: It is the product of 28 and 6.

7. Calin knows that a Category 4 hurricane can be between 131 – 155 mph. Find the difference between the two speeds.

8. Mr. Harold and Ms. Gail bought 16 pieces of plywood. Each piece cost $6.90. How much did they spend on plywood?

9. The town was under a hurricane warning for a total of 18 hours. Convert this to minutes.

10. Steven left his house and drove to a safer location. He drove 110 miles, but it took him 4 hours to get there because of the traffic. What was his average speed?

Jeopardy

Directions: Read the clue. Answer in the form of a question using the math terms.

1. a five-sided figure—Ex. What is a _____ ?
2. the difference between the highest and the lowest number—What is the _____ ?
3. 1000 years—
4. another word for average—
5. the bottom part of a fraction—
6. information that has been gathered—
7. 3.14 x diameter—
8. 100 years—
9. a small unit of length in the Metric System—
10. a numerator over a denominator—
11. the distance around an object—
12. the answer to a division problem—
13. the answer when you add numbers together—
14. the chance of something happening—
15. the answer you get when you multiply numbers together—
16. a number that represents the middle value of a group of numbers—
17. train tracks are—
18. a 2-D shape with 3 angles and 3 straight sides—
19. the answer when you subtract—
20. a number that is divisible by only 1 and itself—

Word Bank

sum	data	prime number
difference	denominator	parallel
product	pentagon	century
quotient	triangle	range
perimeter	fraction	probability
average	mean	circumference
centimeter	millennium	

Keeping Up with the Skills

1. A scooter will cost James $58.00. How many can James buy for $406.00?

2. How many brownies are in each box if 42 boxes have a total of 756 brownies.

3. Farmer Greg earned $9,452.00 when he sold his 6 cows.
    How much did Greg earn from each cow?

4. Michael watched videos from 6:48 PM until 9:25 PM. During this time he saw 3 videos. The first video lasted 40 minutes, and the second video lasted 75 minutes. How long did the third video last?

5. If 6 identical books cost $42.00, find the cost of 18 identical books.

6. A building has a perimeter of 90 meters. The length is 26 meters.
    Find the width of the building.

7. The chocolate factory can make 9,240 hearts a day. How many hearts can it make in 5 days?

8. Harold's flight was scheduled to leave at 9:34 AM. It actually left at 10:58 AM. How late was the flight?

9. A businesswoman spent 3 nights at a hotel. She paid $137.00 each night. How much was her hotel bill?

10. Megan had a 9.5 hour long flight from Germany to Atlanta.
    The plane averaged 575 miles per hour. Approximately how far did Megan fly?

11. Conner's Lawn Service earns $42.50 for each lawn they cut.
    The company averages 5 lawns a day, and they work 6 days a week.
    How much should the company earn in a week?

Maintenance Department

1. The average of four classes is 22 students. The first class has 22 students, the second class has 24 students, and the third class has 30 students. How many students are in the fourth class?

2. Jacob has a camper that is 30 feet long and 12 feet wide. Find the perimeter and the area of the camper.

3. It is 11:00 AM now. Ed has a dental appointment in 5 hours. What time is his appointment?

4. Moyuru sent out 28 invitations. Twenty people responded. What percent of the people responded to his invitation?

5. The nail got hit 41 times the first minute, 82 times the second minute, and 123 times the third minute. At this rate, how many times did the nail get hit the fourth minute?

6. Anton's science experiment called for 8.28 ml of oil and 16.56 ml of water. How much more water does he need than oil?

7. Mark was born in 1960. Paul was born in 1962. Gail was born in 1964, and Steven was born in 1968. Write 4 facts using the information.
    a)
    b)
    c)
    d)

8. We are two mystery numbers. Our sum is 17, and our product is 72. Who are we?

9. Give the missing addend. $75 + G = 94$

10. One boy weighed 23 kg, and another boy weighed 18 kilograms. The boys weighed _____ kg together. Convert this to pounds by multiplying the total number of kg by 2.2 pounds.

Our Nation

1. There are 50 states in the United States. Factor 50 into prime numbers.

2. The U.S. Constitution was adopted on September 17, 1787.
   How long have we used the Constitution?

3. The world's strongest surface wind was recorded at Mount Washington, New Hampshire at 231 mph. Find the sum and the product of the digits.

4. The world's oldest tree is in California. It is about 4,700 years old!
   Round the number to the nearest thousand.

5. The tallest tree in the United States is 367.5 feet tall!
   Convert this to inches. Convert the height of the tree to yards.

6. The highest recorded temperature was 134 F in Death Valley, CA.
   The lowest recorded temperature was – 80 F in Alaska.
   Find the difference in the two temperatures.

7. The longest U.S. River System is the Missouri-Mississippi.
   It is about 3,708 miles long. Divide this number by 2.

8. The pilgrims arrived in 1620 aboard the Mayflower. How many years ago was that?

9. There were 13 original colonies. Finish the pattern.
   13, 26, 39, _____, _____, _____, _____, _____

10. In 1565 the first permanent European settlement was established in St. Augustine, Florida. Explain why 1565 is an odd number.

11. In 1776 the colonies declared independence from Britain.
    Is 1776 evenly divisible by 3?

12. George Washington was elected President in 1789. Abraham Lincoln was elected in 1860. Find the difference.

13. In 1920, women were given the right to vote under the 19th amendment to the Constitution. Multiply 1,920 by 19 to find the product.

14. Between the years 1929-1933, approximately 13 million people lost their jobs during the Great Depression. Write this number using digits.

15. Martin Luther King, Jr., a black civil rights leader, was assassinated in 1968. Explain why 1968 in an even number.

16. There are 50 stars on our flag. List all the factors of 50.

17. Presidential elections are held every four years. Finish the pattern.
    2008   2012   2016   _____   _____ _____

18. The Grand Canyon gets up to 15 miles across and has a length of about 277 miles. Using these measurements, what would an approximate perimeter be for the Grand Canyon?

19. The Gateway Arch in St. Louis, Missouri is 630 feet tall and 630 feet wide. Find the product of the two numbers.

20. The distance between Miami, FL and Seattle, WA is about 3,336 miles! A person has 7 days to drive there.
    What is the average mileage per day?

21. A major earthquake struck San Francisco in 1906.
    Hurricane Katrina hit New Orleans and other areas in 2005.
    How many years apart were these two natural disasters?

Path to Understanding

1. Danielle saw 9 horses. She gave each horse 11 apples.
   How many apples did she give to the horses?

2. Nick had 15 spelling words. He wrote each of them 5 times.
   How many words did Nick write in all?

3. Jim read where a man ate 7 pizzas. Each pizza was cut into eight pieces.
   How many pieces of pizza did the man eat?

4. Melody has $20.50. She sees a CD she wants for $12.99.
   How much money will she have left if she buys the CD?

5. Britney made 23 shots at basketball. Her dad made 31 shots.
   Find the sum, difference and the average of the two numbers.

6. Russell went down the hill 9 times. Each ride took 2.5 minutes.
   How long did he ride?

7. Alexander loves chocolate chip cookies! He ate 4 on Friday, 8 Saturday, and he ate 12 on
   Sunday. How many cookies will he eat on Monday if he follows this pattern?

8. Devin called 7 people on the telephone. He talked with each person approximately 4
   minutes. Estimate how long he talked on the phone.

9. Mrs. C. bought 3 bottles of soda. Each soda was $1.15. How much was spent on soda?

10. Nathan saw 56 pieces of pie. He was asked to divide them evenly among 4 trays. Nathan
    put _____ on each tray.

11. Monica brought in 120 pencils. She divided them evenly among 10 students. Each
    student received how many pencils?

12. Alexander used 1/4 of his 60 band aids. How many did he use?

Popcorn Sales

Popcorn Prices: $50, $40, $30, $20, $15, $15, $13, $13 and $8

1. Mrs. Kinney spent $28.00 on popcorn. List the possible combinations.

2. Calin sold $348.00 worth of popcorn. Approximately 70% of his sales will go to the local Scouting chapter. How much of Calin's sales will go to pay for the popcorn? How much will be given to his Scouting chapter?

3. Sara is a very smart buyer! Help her figure out which is a better buy.
   Is a $15.00 26 oz. Gourmet popcorn a better deal or is an $8.00 11 oz.
   Gourmet popcorn a better deal? Explain your answer.

4. Steven's phone number on the form was 585-2411. Add each digit to find the sum. Multiply each digit to find the product.

5. Two out of sixteen people prepaid for their popcorn. Reduce this fraction. Find the percentage of people who prepaid.

6. The prices for the tins of popcorn are $50, $40, $30, $20, $15, $15, $13, $13 and $8.
   a) Find the range for the prices.
   b) Find the mean/average cost.
   c) What is the mode (occurs most often)?

7. Calin sold $348.00 worth of popcorn to 16 people. What is the quotient if you divide 348 by 16?

8. Paul owed $35.00 for the popcorn. List three combinations of bills Paul could give to Calin.

9. Calin looked at his order sheet. He saw the numbers 2,1,3,4,1,6, and 9.
   List at least six facts about the number 2,134,169.

10. Factor $348.00 into prime numbers using a factor tree!

Scientific Facts

1. A year is the amount of time it takes Earth to make one whole revolution around the sun. There are 365 days in a year. Factor 365 into prime numbers.

2. Water makes up approximately 70% of the Earth's surface.
Write 70% in decimal form.

3. Aristotle was a famous Greek scientist and philosopher. He believed the best way to understand nature was by observing it. Aristotle was born in 384 BC. How long ago was this?

4. Charles Darwin lived from 1809-1882. He is famous for his ideas on natural selection and evolution. How long did he live?

5. The fastest land animal is the cheetah. It can run close to seventy miles per hour. List all the factors of 70.

6. The freezing point of pure water is 32 F. Continue the pattern.
    32   64   96   128   _____   _____   _____

7. The atomic number for zinc is 30. List all the factors of 30.

8. The Great Barrier Reef near Australia is the longest coral reef.
It is about 1,243 miles long. Divide this number by 2.

9. Mount McKinley, the highest peak in North America, is about 20,320 feet high. Convert this to inches.

10. The Pacific Ocean's average depth is approximately 14,130 feet.
A lake in Russia has a depth of 5,315 feet. Find the difference.

11. Oxygen makes up about 21.5 % of the air we breathe. Nitrogen accounts for about 78% of it. What percentage of the air we breathe is something else?

Taking Flight

Directions: Use the chart to answer the following questions.
The prices are based on a round trip from St. Louis.

Destination	Price
Atlanta	$476
Boston	$482
Chicago	$218
Dallas	$390
Denver	$625
Las Vegas	$279
Los Angeles	$580
Miami	$424
Philadelphia	$386
Washington, DC	$376

1. Ouri wants to go to the cheapest destination. Where should he go?

2. Danielle and Nicole want to fly to Miami, Florida. How much will they spend on tickets?

3. Travis has $375.00 in his savings account. How much more does he need if he wants to go to Dallas?

4. Ryan lives in Washington, DC and Dean lives in Denver. If Tawna is watching her budget, who should she visit?

5. Andrea and her two sisters are planning a skiing trip to Denver.
How much will they spend on three tickets?

6. A family of 4 flew to Los Angeles. A family of 6 flew to Chicago. Which family spent the least amount of money on airline tickets?

7. Lillian wants to fly home once a month to see her parents.
Her parents live in Miami. How much can she expect to spend a year?

The Class Trip

1. The clerk at the hotel told Mrs. Slane he forgot some of the room numbers. He knew a room was 24 and another was 28. Follow this pattern. What are the next five room numbers?

2. Kelsey bought a square pizza. Each side measured 3.7 cm. What was the perimeter of her pizza? What was the area of her pizza?

3. Maya and Athene wanted a snack on the train. Maya ate 3/4 of her pizza. Athene ate 4/9 of her pizza. Who ate more? Explain how you got your answer.

4. William was being very good in Rome. Mrs. Slane told him she would buy him a triple scoop cone if he could multiply and reduce the following fractions. Help him! 15/20 x 25/30 =

5. David bought 2 pizzas. William bought 3. P.J. ate 1/3 of David's pizza. Chris ate 2/9 of William's pizza. How much pizza was eaten? How much pizza was left over?

6. Ziggy was locked in his hotel room. The manager said he must make at least three equivalent fractions for 3/4 before he could get the spare key. What are some possibilities?

7. Twenty 6th graders were leaving the train station at 4:55 PM. They were to be there by 4:40 PM. Two-fifths were early. How many were early? How many were late? How many were on time?

8. Mrs. Boit bought five students an ice-cream cone. The students had a 3 scoop, a 4 scoop, a 5 scoop, a 6 scoop and a 7 scoop. What was the average number of scoops?

9. Steffani was glad there were only five people in her room, not 4R=32!
   R= _____

10. Oliver stepped on one of the Spanish Steps in Rome. It measured 3.5 meters by 8.5 meters. Find the perimeter and area of the step.

11. Corey and Vilma wanted to answer this Roman riddle. Help them!
    List all the factors of thirty or take the chance of getting dirty!

12. Mark and his classmates went to sleep at 10:00 PM. They slept for 7 hours and 19 minutes. What time did they wake up?

13. A mystery student, not to be named here to protect his/her identity, had $200.00. The student spent $194.99 of the money on the trip.
How much did he/she return home with?

14. Miho spent $146.79 in Rome. What number is in the hundredths place?

15. Andrew and Jessica heard there were 1,000 people on the train.
They knew that 125 of them were from their school. Reduce this fraction. What percentage of the people were from their school?

16. The weather was going to be very weird during the trip. The high was going to be 82 F, and the low was expected to dip to 48 F. What will be the difference in temperature?

17. Lauren and Jackie read the Italian Lottery was tonight! In order to win money they had to factor 625 into prime numbers. Help them.

18. Mr. Kline said the hotel phone number was 245-471-4400. What would the product be if he multiplied all three numbers?

19. Mrs. Kussman and Mrs. Rhodes found two stones. One was shaped like a pentagon. One was shaped like an octagon. Find the sum, difference and the product of the two numbers. List all the factors of the product.
Factor the product into prime numbers.

20. Mrs. Dalley and Mr. Phillips told their groups that this section of the road to Rome was 15 km long. They wanted to know if the kids could divide 15 km into four equal pieces. Could the kids do it? What is the correct answer?

21. Mr. Lawler learned a lot about the class. After all, he had spent many hours with them. If he was with them from Sunday evening at 4:55 PM until the next Saturday at 11:46 AM, how long had he spent with them?

22. Mrs. Muller-Rust wore a Roman toga. Only 1/4 of the toga was cotton.
What percentage of her toga was made from silk? Can you be sure?
Explain your answer.

23. Mrs. Friday found a piece of real Italian spaghetti that was 925 cm long!
She divided it evenly into 25 pieces. How long was each piece?

24. Mrs. Dalley and Mr. Porterfield ate 3/4 of an Italian dessert. Write five equivalent fractions for 3/4.

25. Steve, Calin and Sara all needed a lot of band-aids because of their blisters. Steve needed 7, Calin needed 49 and Sara needed 343! How many would Paul need if he followed this pattern?

26. Patrick's mom, Sophia's mom and Maduri's dad each bought a book about Rome. Each book was $13.95. What is the total cost?

27. A mystery man spent $69.31 on 29 ice creams. How much was each?

28. The class arrived at the hotel at 9:50 AM. Mr. Brown said that they had 35 minutes to freshen up before departing at what time?

29. Jayshree read where the plane is 8 m by 27 m. Find the perimeter.
    Find the area.

30. Alex ate 3 10/12 pieces of pizza. Maduri ate only 2 1/2 pieces. Find the sum. Find the difference.

31. This mystery person talked 57% of the 180 minutes he/she was on the bus. How many minutes did this person talk out of 180 minutes?

32. There were 1,000 strings of spaghetti in the bowl. The boys sitting at the table ate 38% of them. How many strings of spaghetti were eaten?

33. Federica ran around the hotel 17 times. It took three minutes each time.
    How long did it take her to run around 17 times? How long would it take her to run around 25 times at this rate?

Friendly Math Reminders

Average/Mean
1st: Find the sum of all the numbers.
2nd: Divide the sum by the total number of numbers.

Circumference C = 3.14 x Diameter

Mean—the average of a set of numbers

Median—the middle number when all of the numbers are in order from the lowest to the highest

Mode—the number that occurs the most often

Measurement Review
1 foot = 12 inches
1 yard = 3 feet
1 mile = 5,280 feet
1 pound = 16 ounces
1 ton = 2,000 pounds
1 gallon = 4 quarts
1 cm = 10 mm
1 meter = 100 cm
1 km = 1,000 m

Percentages—To find a percentage of a number, turn the percentage into a decimal. Ex. 75% of 60 = .75 x 60 = 45

Perimeter, Area and Volume
Perimeter—the distance around a figure (add all sides)
Area—the number of square units needed to cover a figure (length x width)
Volume—a measurement of how much space something takes up (length x width x height)

Prime Number—a number divisible by 1 and itself only Ex. 29, 37, 59, 73, etc.

Notes

Answer Key

Add it Up

1) 76 students
2) 437 students
3) 420 marbles
4) less than
5) 606 tickets
6) $5.04
7) 90 cookies
8) 84 things
9) $26.44
10) 482 sheets
11) $64.40

What's the Difference

1) 81 people
2) $2.71
3) 760 pounds
4) $.35
5) 296 bananas
6) $141.47
7) $10.24
8) 14 candy bars
9) 269 kg, 328 kg
10) 13 cars
11) $45.25
12) $310.18

Giving and Taking Away

1) 281 lbs. & 131 lbs.
2) $13.42 & $1.58
3) 35 hours & 20 minutes
4) $39.56 & yes
5) $29.43 & $2.55
6) $4.83 $ $5.17
7) 694 kg & Metric
8) 2,144 toys
9) $74.62 & $25.38
10) 55 movies

11) 4,114 miles & 1,314 miles
12) 67 bites
13) 623 students & 45 boys
14) 41 boys & 77 students
15) 1,653 miles

Multiplication . . .
Speedy Addition

1) 510 pieces
2) 1,470 marbles
3) 71 inches
4) 5 pies
5) $161.25
6) 157.48 cm
7) 2,160 holes
8) $180.93
9) 336 lbs.
10) $252.00
11) 225 minutes

Multiplication Madness

1) 2,063 times
2) 378 pieces
3) $27.40
4) 140 treats
5) $93.00
6) no & 2,445
7) 10,260 buds
8) $147.50
9) 42 cars
10) 2,940 calories
11) 3,850 oz.
12) 3,900 scoops
13) 6,330 ants
14) 84,000 miles
15) 280 fans
16) 175,242 lbs.
17) 9,125 pages

18) $681.10
19) $4,396.40
20) $1,095.00
21) 90 hours
22) 2,058

A Great Product

1) 2,190 leaves
2) 156 cookies
3) $1,875.00
4) 390 pieces & $877.50
5) 60 miles
6) $174.00
7) 44, 22 & 11
8) $4,055.00
9) 990 minutes
10) 630 papers
11) 520 miles
12) $300.00

Dividing it Up

1) 288 oz.
2) 5 buses
3) 99 entries
4) 3 people
5) $.67
6) $6.35
7) 8 pieces
8) 15 cookies
9) $5.89
10) 14 pieces & 2 inches
11) $13.00
12) 12 balloons
13) quotient
14) 1,611 mi. & 179 mi.
15) 19 pages & 5
16) 24 students
17) 64 students

18) 5 pencils
19) no & 50 groups
20) 23 problems
21) 74 weeks & 2 cookies
22) 3 mysteries

Part Time
1) 30 apples
2) 5 Gummi Bears
3) 15 miles/day
4) 4 feet 6 inches
5) 23 problems
6) 5 cookies
7) approx. 19 hours
8) 412 yards
9) 14 rolls
10) 25 stamps
11) 13 books
12) 312 names

Just Average
1) 427 cars
2) 75.16%
3) 780 pages & 260 pages
4) 42.5 pencils
5) 80 pieces & 16/day
6) $532.00 & $177.33
7) 94%
8) 107 min. & 35.6 min.
9) 349 kg
10) 5 scoops

What Do You Mean
1) 30 years old
2) 52.46 mph
3) 77 & 19.25 bananas
4) 80%
5) 45 pages
6) 5 hotdogs
7) 102 pages & 25.5/day
8) 2,460 & 492 calories
9) 69
10) 72.6 seconds
11) 53 cookies
12) 36

I Get the Point
1) 2.8 miles
2) 27 mpg
3) 1,932.8 m
4) $7.55
5) 28.5 mpg
6) $87.50
7) $.29
8) $7.20
9) $3.68
10) 25 pencils
11) $3.90, $3.22 & Debbie

Fractions . . . A Part of a Solution
1) 2 1/3 cookies
2) $18.60
3) 23/24
4) yes
5) 33/50
6) various answers
7) 1/16 tsp
8) 3/4 cup per bowl
9) 26 books
10) 16 trees
11) 172 vehicles

Fantastic Fractions
1) 10 3/10 cookies
2) 2 2/5 cake
3) 5/8 & 3/8
4) 10 7/10 pizza
5) 13 5/6 eggs
6) 2/8 glass
7) 1/3 concertos
8) 2 1/3 pizza
9) 6 1/2 inches
10) $20.00 & $4.00
11) 1/3
12) $1.35 to charity
13) 3/10 & 7/10
14) various answers
15) Christopher's horse
16) playing

17) 2 cups sugar, 1 1/3 cups butter, 4 eggs, 3 cups flour, 1 1/2 tsp vanilla
18) 2 1/4
19) various answers
20) Example: 16/21
21) 1/3 blueberry, 2/3 not
22) 2/5 lasagna

Let's Have a Piece
1) 8/10 & 4/5
2) Jon
3) 2 1/3 miles
4) 16/20 & 80%
5) 12 2/3 cups
6) 18 children
7) 8 7/20
8) 5/8 kg
9) 15 stars
10) 11 1/12 & 1 7/12
11) 12 players
12) 30 girls & 20 boys
13) 8 5/8 pizza
14) 6 3/4 inches
15) 7/8 cup
16) 7/8 chicken
17) 5/6 day
18) no
19) 2 3/4 cake
20) 5/6 day
21) 21/24

Measurement Matters
1) P=52 ft. & A=88 ft. sq.
2) 32 in.
3) 7 km
4) 20,000 cm
5) P=140 ft & A=1,000 ft. sq.
6) 12 ft.
7) 75.36 in.
8) 31.40 in.
9) 21 yards & 756 in.
10) 32 degrees
11) 378 yards & 2 feet
12) 12 ft.
13) 14 ft. by 20 ft.

14) 24 in. & 75.36 in.

15) 28.26 in & 56.52 in. & 16 people

16) P=84m & A=392 m sq.

17) yes

18) 25 ft. by 12 ft.

19) P=24 in. & A=36 in. sq.

20) 189 cm

21) 11,000 pounds

Undercover

1) 742

2) 7,839

3) 1,230

4) 5 & 8

5) 5 & 6

6) 4 & 16

7) 37

8) C=12

9) 12 & 14

10) 6 & 17

11) x = 9

12) 96%

13) 8

Solve it

1) 3 & 8

2) 5 & 9

3) 4 & 6

4) 9 & 16

5) 6 & 8

6) 4 & 9

7) 14 & 28

8) 7 & 8

9) 3 & 36

10) 12 & 21

11) 14 & 15

Popular Percentages

1) 160 students

2) 4/5 & 40 answers

3) 29,750 & 12,750 votes

4) $3,150.00

5) $.52 & $13.47

6) 70%

7) $16.80 & $39.20

8) 82 & 2

9) 24%

10) 75%

11) 9 children

12) 2,304 flowers

13) 935 mi. & 765 mi.

14) 6 hours

15) 216 minutes

16) 9 days

17) $29.94

18) 3/20

19) 24 students

20) 20% of flights

21) 140 houses

22) 66%

23) 80%

A Part of it

1) 270 pieces

2) 12 & 8 colleges

3) 1,152 minutes

4) 79%

5) $152.35

6) $125.00

7) $4.13

8) 86%

9) $65.40

10) 11 & 33 papers

11) 200 cookies

12) 3 cookies

It's About Time

1) 11:10 AM

2) 45 & 315 minutes

3) 4:37 PM

4) 2 hours & 15 minutes

5) 1 hour & 52 min.

6) 2 hours & 40 min.

7) 3:45 PM

8) $13.50

9) 1 hour & 7 min.

10) 2 days & 5 hours

11) 8,100 seconds

12) 10 hours & 35 min.

Time Out

1) 585 min. & 10 hours

2) 14 hours & 25 min.

3) 5 hours & 21 min.

4) 3:30 AM

5) 2:00 PM, 5:00 PM, etc.

6) 4 hours & 40 min.

7) 7 hours & 15 min.

8) 4 hours & 56 min.

9) 323 min.

10) 49 hours, 3,000 min. and 2 days & 4 hours

11) 6:45 PM

12) 1:08 PM

13) 6:23, 6:31 etc.

14) 4 1/2 hours

15) 8 hours & 34 min.

16) 135 min. & 8,100 sec.

17) 17 hours & 30 min.

18) 15 hours & 22 min.

19) approx. 11 minutes

20) 12 hours

21) 75 mph & 900 miles

22) 49 hours & 2,555 hours/yr.

23) 80 minutes

24) 3:30 PM

A Bit More Challenging

1) 156 times

2) various answers

3) 7 years old

4) 8 combinations

5) yes

6) 33 points

7) 52 & 10

8) same time

9) 1984, etc.

10) odd number

11) 208

12) H, M, P, G, S

13) yes

14) 4 bags of tomatoes & 3 bags of corn

15) 6 horses & 9 ducks

16) 1, 2, 5, 10, 25, 50

17) 6 dogs

18) 120 boxes
19) 33 degrees

We've Got Problems
1) $23.34
2) 8 hours & 9 min.
3) $1,400,987.01
4) 13 min. & 10 sec.
5) $14,938.56
6) 800 pages
7) GCF = 14
8) $65.70
9) 614 eggs
10) 252 & 288 boxes
11) 2 1/4
12) 80%
13) 30 liters
14) excuse, my & Sally
15) 345-7108
16) $48.88
17) 9 eggs
18) 8 5/8
19) 18 cookies
20) 900 marshmallows
21) 225 cookies
22) $5.95
23) 2 hours & 27 min.

A Little Bit of Everything
1) 36 min.
2) 7 1/2, 6tsp., 3 tsp., 1 1/2 tsp., 3 cups, 3 3/4 cups, 6 eggs, 3tsp., 6TB & 3 tsp.
3) 57 hours
4) 14 rows
5) 232,344 words
6) $668.42
7) 68.6
8) 33 & 20,736
9) $5.46
10) 5x5x5x2
11) 591.5 hours
12) 130
13) 5.2 or 5 R1
14) 342,994 & 67,424
15) 70% & 30%

16) 741,137
17) 3x2x2x2x2x2
18) $25.50
19) 3,933 m
20) 6 & 12
21) 6 foreign cars
22) 300 calories
23) 13 doughnuts

Mixing it Up
1) 12, $1.20 & $.63
2) $5.25
3) $1,208.33
4) $4.75, $4.85 7 $4.80
5) 37 jugs
6) 56 min.
7) $.48 & $4.80
8) $109.65
9) 240 blackberries
10) 28 girls
11) 800 words
12) $340.00
13) 24 cm. & 75.36 cm
14) $90.00
15) 88%
16) 67%
17) 5/26 & no
18) P=120 ft. & A=875 ft. sq.
19) 6 ft. by 9 ft.
20) 42.5
21) 32
22) $824.84
23) various answers

Around the House
1) 19 pieces
2) $22.76 savings
3) 1/10
4) 163, 21 & 6,532
5) 2x2x2x3x5x7
6) $.46, $.40 &$.40
7) $8.75
8) $20.50
9) 60 troops
10) 11 hours & 13 min.
11) 2 5/12 yards

12) 512 pieces
13) 588 eggs
14) 9 2/9
15) 12 1/4 doughnuts
16) $13.35
17) 13 hours & 46 min.
18) 13 yards
19) 1/26
20) 300 envelopes
21) $15.30
22) $49.36
23) $.12

Back to School
1) $.33
2) $1.98
3) $3.51
4) 192 pictures
5) 1 hour & 23 minutes
6) $81.18
7) $.83
8) $.44
9) $2.62
10) 9 things
11) P=80 ft. & A=300 ft. sq.
12) 20 feet
13) $57.73
14) 28 min.
15) 280 min.
16) 83%
17) 123 miles
18) P=50 in
A= 154 in. sq.
V= 1,694 in. cubed
19) 1/4
20) $42.00
21) 45 quizzes
22) 20 & 576
23) $295.26

Daily Dose
1) 25.12 cm
2) 5 7/12
3) 25%
4) 2x3x5x5x5
5) 66 inches

6) yes 1/4 of deck
7) $1.40
8) 3x3x5x5
9) 300 ft. cubed
10) 176 pages
11) 9.85
12) 148 containers
13) 75 seconds
14) 70 units
15) yes
16) $.40
17) $4,914.00
18) 108 ft. sq.
19) $.70
20) tire
21) 8 hours
22) $6.95
23) 75 seconds
24) 8:15 AM

Food for Thought
1) 21 people
2) 32 candies
3) 144 pieces
4) $111.00
5) $16.32
6) $17.50 & $13.00
7) 8.5 lbs. & 1.5 lbs.
8) 57 pumpkins
9) 433 ft. & 4 inches
10) 16 pounds
11) 7 boxes
12) $2.78 & $55.60
13) $2.07, $6.27 & yes
14) 9 hours
15) 9 dozen
16) 850 calories
17) 168 oz.
18) 18 cups
19) 5,120 bits

Holiday Story Problems
1) 288 & 336 snowballs
2) 3 more reindeer
3) 42 cookies
4) 23 pieces

5) 96 cookies
6) 576 ornaments & no
7) 132 marshmallows
8) 177,677 miles
9) 4 hours & 11 min.
10) 1962.4 per hour
11) 195
12) 70 & 17.5 candy canes
13) $346.00
14) greater than,
   P=72 m
   A=288 m. sq.
15) $270.00
16) 8 pieces
17) 1,470 sec. & 24.5 min.
18) $8,172.00
19) 40 not broken
20) 30 times, 84 & 21
21) 1:30 PM
22) 2 hours & 11 minutes

It's a Hurricane
1) 58 mph
2) 18 mph
3) 4,238 people
4) $15.00
5) 7 trailers
6) 168 mph
7) 24 mph
8) $110.40
9) 1,080 minutes
10) 27.5 mph

Jeopardy
1) pentagon
2) range
3) millennium
4) mean
5) denominator
6) data
7) circumference
8) century
9) centimeter
10) fraction
11) perimeter
12) quotient

13) sum
14) probability
15) product
16) average
17) parallel
18) triangle
19) difference
20) prime number

Keeping Up With Skills
1) 7 scooters
2) 18 brownies
3) $1,575.33
4) 42 minutes
5) $126.00
6) 19 meters
7) 46,200 hearts
8) 1 hour & 24 min. late
9) $411.00
10) 5,462.5 miles
11) $1,275.00

Maintenance Department
1) 12 students
2) P=84 ft. & A=360 ft. sq.
3) 4:00 PM
4) 71%
5) 164 times
6) 8.28 ml
7) various answers
8) 8 & 9
9) G = 19
10) 90.2 lbs.

Our Nation
1) 2x5x5
2) various answers
3) 6 & 6
4) 5,000 years
5) 4,410 in. & 122.5 yds.
6) 214 degrees
7) 1,854 miles
8) various answers
9) 52, 65, 78, 91 & 104
10) 5 is an odd number
11) yes & 592

12) 71 years
13) 36,480
14) 13,000,000
15) It ends with an 8.
16) 1, 2, 5, 10, 25, 50
17) 2020, 2024, 2028
18) approx. 584 miles
19) 396,900
20) 476.5 miles/day
21) 99 years

Path to Understanding
1) 99 apples
2) 75 times
3) 56 pizzas
4) $7.51
5) 54, 8 & 27 shots
6) 22.5 min
7) 16 cookies
8) 28 min.
9) $3.45
10) 14 pieces
11) 12 pencils
12) 15 band aids

Popcorn Sales
1) $13 & $15, $20 & $8
2) $104.40 & $243.60
3) $15.00
4) 26 & 1,600
5) 12.5%
6) $42.00, $22.67 mean - $13 & $15
7) 21.75 or 21 R12
8) various answers
9) various answers
10) 3x2x2x29

Scientific Facts
1) 5x73
2) .70
3) various answers
4) 73 years
5) 1, 2, 5, 7, 10, 14, 35 & 70
6) 160, 192, 224
7) 1, 2, 3, 5, 6, 10, 15 & 30

8) 621.5 miles
9) 243,840 inches
10) 8,815 feet
11) .5

Taking Flight
1) Chicago
2) $848.00
3) $15.00
4) Ryan
5) $1,875.00
6) family of 6
7) $5,088.00

The Class Trip
1) 32, 36, 40, 44, 48
2) P=14.8 cm & A=13.69 cm sq.
3) Maya
4) 5/8
5) 5/9 & 4 4/9
6) various answers
7) 8 students
8) 5 scoops
9) R= 8
10) P=24 m & A=29.75 m sq.
11) 1, 2, 3, 5, 6, 10, 15 & 30
12) 5:19 AM
13) $5.01
14) 9
15) 1/8 & 12.5%
16) 34 degrees
17) 5x5x5x5
18) 507,738,000
19) 13, 3, 40
Factors: 1, 2, 4, 5, 8, 10, 20 & 40
5x2x2x2
20) 3.75 km
21) 138 hours & 51 min.
22) not enough info.
23) 37 cm
24) various answers
25) 2,401 band aids
26) $41.85
27) $2.39
28) 10:25 AM
29) P=70 m & A=216 m sq.

30) 6 1/3 & 1 1/3
31) 102.6 minutes
32) 380 strings
33) 51 & 75 minutes